Closer

to

You

A Devotional for Dads & Daughters

Timothy and Sarah Sloan

FREILING
PUBLISHING

Published by Freiling Publishing,
a division of Freiling Agency, LLC.

P.O. Box 1264
Warrenton, VA 20188

www.FreilingPublishing.com

HB ISBN: 978-1-956267-91-4
PB ISBN: 978-1-956267-95-2
eBook ISBN: 978-1-956267-92-1

Printed in the United States of America

Dedicated to Soren Grace, who shares the love of Dad as a daughter and God, our Father!

Contents

Section 4
Family

Section 5
Growing Up

Acknowledgments

WE ARE GRATEFUL to everyone who has been a part of this writing process. We can't thank Tom Freiling and the Freiling Publishing team enough for believing in us. They made us feel like a success before one word was written and throughout the process.

Thank you to our family, who supported us every step of the way. Our love for them knows no limit. Sonya, Timothy's wife and Sarah's mom, is the glue that holds our family together. She was our biggest cheerleader in completing this project. Soren Grace and Timothy John shared this entire journey with us. They encouraged their sister and supported their dad every step of the way.

Thank you to our family of faith, The Luke Church. You've always given us room to grow and discover our purpose. We couldn't ask for a better community of believers to do life with.

Lastly, this project is the result of the urging of Ms. Ivy McGregor. After speaking at an event at our church, she pulled us aside and said we should write a dad-and-daughter book together. We are incredibly grateful for her encouragement and discernment that night. We pray that this book glorifies God and helps build stronger relationships between dads and daughters.

Introduction

THIS DEVOTIONAL WAS a heart project that we wrote together. Originally it was meant to be a way for us to grow closer together, and also in God. But as we talked about each devotional and began to pray with each other, we decided that other dads and daughters might also be encouraged by our words. That's how this book happened!

The dad-daughter relationship is very important and special, and even research shows that the well-fathered daughter is the most likely to have relationships with men that are emotionally intimate and fulfilling. At the same time, dads can learn a lot about life from their own daughters. They say that "a girl's first true love is her dad." A daughter's love gives a dad confidence, hope, and so much joy.

So we pray that this devotional will help you, dad and daughter, to grow closer together, closer to our heavenly Father...and to help you both dream big!

Section 1

Communication

1

Closer to You

Draw near to God,
and he will draw near to you.
(James 4:8 ESV)

I Am Here

WHEN MY DAUGHTER was born and through her toddler and elementary-age years, it was simpler to show her that I was "there" for her. Holding her, playing with a toy or doll, or even holding her hand and taking a walk were all simple ways I could express my love for her.

But when our daughters begin to grow into young women, I have discovered that I need to be more intentional in the ways I express my love for her. It's a lot like how we should tend to our relationship with God. It's not enough to just "show up" with God. We need to spend purposeful time in prayer and devotion in our walk with the Lord, and we need to make it a habit, not an empty ritual. We can't expect to build a real relationship with God if we approach Him flippantly or without an open heart. I believe the more time we spend with God, the more He will be involved in our lives.

Likewise, dads need to spend quality time with their daughters and listen to them with intentionality and sincerity. Our relationship will be closer when we continually show our daughters that "I am here for you."

Drawing Nearer

IF YOU WANT to get closer to something, you must move forward. You have to step toward your goal to achieve it. My relationship with my dad is like this. For it to grow, it has to be nurtured. For it to thrive, I have to invest in it.

My dad has modeled this for me in his relationship with his heavenly Father. He is intentional in spending time with God. He reads his Bible, prays, worships, and surrounds himself with Christian fellowship. He draws near to God, and an anointing is evident in that.

As a daughter, I have learned from my dad that to have a relationship with him, I must intentionally draw closer, investing my time in conversation and connection with him. It is essential that I do this with my heavenly Father as well, growing closer to God as I draw nearer to Him.

What distracts a dad and daughter
from growing closer together?

2

Dialogue

When the cares of my heart are many,
your consolations cheer my soul.
(Psalm 94:19 ESV)

What's on Your Mind?

SPENDING TIME WITH God isn't about gaining more knowledge. Our faith is more than a set of beliefs. It's about building a relationship. It's about getting to know Him as real as the person next to us, yet as mysterious as the universe. And it isn't until we enter into a real relationship with God that we can expect Him to be an integral part of our lives.

What does this mean for our relationships with our daughters? We can't expect our daughters to listen to and open up with us if we don't spend time building the relationship. When we ask our daughters, "what's on your mind?" they might want to tell us, but if we're too busy for the relationship, they won't be honest or forthcoming. Trust comes before honesty.

My daughter is bold in her interactions with me. Daughters often are bold! But if we push them off or aren't attentive to them, our closeness with them will eventually lessen, just like it does with God when we aren't attentive to Him. We want our daughters to ask for our opinions and to get our input, just like God wants to hear from us too!

Can We Talk?

"DAD, CAN WE talk?" I would nervously ask while awaiting a response. Asking my dad to talk about something serious always brought a bit of anxiety with it. *What would he say? How would he react?* I wanted his advice but was intimidated to talk with him.

I think that is the funny thing about relationships: whether with your dad or with God, you have to open the door first. Dialogue requires initiation, sometimes from the parent and sometimes from the child, but someone has to step up and start the conversation.

When we want to talk to God, we have to engage—whether in prayer or in simply opening the Bible and reading God's Word. The same thing is true of our dads. When we have something serious weighing on our hearts, we need to approach our dads with boldness to grow our relationship. It's as simple as asking, can we talk?

How can a dad and daughter go before
God more boldly in prayer?

_____

_____

_____

_____

_____

_____

_____

_____

_____

_____

_____

_____

_____

_____

_____

_____

_____

_____

_____

_____

_____

_____

_____

3

Developing Trust

*You keep him in perfect peace whose mind is
stayed on you because he trusts in you.
(Isaiah 26:3, ESV)*

I Trust You

TRUST IS SOMETHING that becomes more challenging for dads as our daughters grow into young women. It's easy to trust a toddler, or a little girl. But as they grow up and enter a world that we know is full of danger and temptation, our trust in our daughters begins to wane. We love them so much that we fear letting go. It's not that we don't trust our daughters; we don't trust the world!

But it's important that we give our growing daughters the respect they need and deserve. Trust is important in relationships because it allows us both to be more open and giving. If we trust our daughters, and they trust us, we are each more likely, to be honest with each other. At the same time, although our love for our daughters is unconditional, trust sometimes needs to be earned. Our daughters might view trust and freedom as the same thing, but they need to realize trust and freedom are not always the same thing.

This is where prayer comes in. As dads, we need to seek God's wisdom and discernment to know when to trust our daughters and when to be their protector.

I Need to Tell You Something

I HAVE ALWAYS been involved in the dance team and other events in high school. Whether a football game, basketball game, or dance competition, I could always count on my dad to be there. While waiting on stage to perform, I didn't have to see my dad in the crowd to know he was there.

Without fail, my dad could be found sitting in the stands with his camera, recording each performance I participated in. We would later watch the recordings together, and even if I couldn't hear his voice when I was on stage, I could hear it in the recording. I knew that my dad was always there.

Having a dad I could trust helped me understand that I could always trust God to be there for me. Your heavenly Father is always present and available when you need Him. Knowing He's there will give you peace.

How can a dad and daughter learn to trust God
together, even during tough times?

_____

_____

_____

_____

_____

_____

_____

_____

_____

_____

_____

_____

_____

_____

_____

_____

_____

_____

_____

_____

_____

_____

4

Listening

If you have understanding, hear this;
listen to what I say.
(Job 34:16 ESV)

What Did You Say?

SOMETIMES WE DON'T stick with God long enough to hear what He's saying. In the busyness and chaos of our day, we remember to pray but then we jump ahead of Him. We don't listen to what God is trying to tell us, and we forget that He truly wants a relationship with us. In our prayers, we talk to God but then don't listen. We're too busy for a real relationship.

Likewise, your daughter also desires a real relationship with you built on love and listening. Your daughter isn't just looking for solutions. But as a dad, sometimes you may approach your daughter with a quick-fix mentality. You listen, but only briefly, and then you move on to how you can help. You tune her in, then tune her out, not because you don't love your daughter but because you want to "fix" things for her. You forget the importance of listening out of respect for the relationship that she so deeply desires. Your daughter needs conversation. Sometimes she just needs you to listen.

Remember the word "listen" contains the same letters as the word "silent." Acknowledge her presence and just listen. Be present with God and with your daughter.

Do You Hear What I Am Saying?

OFTEN, MY DAD gives me wise instruction, and I internally scoff, thinking he is too old or out of touch to understand or see what I am going through. He tells me something and I choose not to listen, thinking that I know a better way.

I forget that my dad's advice is grounded in experience and God's truth. His wisdom is hard-won based on his own failures and successes. He has lived a whole lot more life than I have, and he sees things that I do not yet see. His instructions are given in love and for my good. However, it is up to me to recognize this and truly listen to him.

Similarly, God is always speaking to us and trying to show us His more excellent way. It takes a lot of humility and growth to listen and learn from His Word. It is not enough just to hear what He says. We have to apply it to our lives, trusting in His guidance.

What can a dad and daughter do together to
better discern God's voice?

_____

_____

_____

_____

_____

_____

_____

_____

_____

_____

_____

_____

_____

_____

_____

_____

_____

_____

_____

_____

_____

_____

_____

5

Honesty

*He who walks blamelessly and does what is right
and speaks truth in his heart.
(Psalm 15:2 ESV)*

I Pinky Promise

WHEN MY DAUGHTER was a small child, she'd make me "pinky promise." She held me to my promises with a clasped finger. It was easy, even cute, when she was a little girl. But the older my daughter gets, the harder it can be to keep my word. The need for honesty in my communication with my daughter is absolutely vital.

We understand the importance of being honest with our heavenly Father. When we give voice to our complaints, our worries, our bitterness, or our fears, we aren't telling God anything that He doesn't already know. We learn to tell God everything. Likewise, your conversations with your daughter also need to be forthright, honest, and full of integrity. Your daughter needs honest conversations, honest feedback, and trustworthy feedback.

Your daughter knows a bait-and-switch when she sees one! She is intuitive as God made her, and she is searching for a relationship that is built on clear and honest communication. She should feel that she can share anything with her dad, just as we can share anything with God. Get gut-level honest with your daughter.

I'm Telling the Truth

OUR HEAVENLY FATHER knows the hearts of His daughters. He sees us completely, and there is nothing that we can hide from Him. He knows all our hurt, fear, shame, and pain, yet He loves us anyway.

Honesty with your dad can be very challenging, especially during your teenage years. You may lie or sneak around because you think you will get away with things or avoid consequences. As a daughter, you may sometimes fear that openness will lead to rejection, punishment, or disapproval. Sometimes you may project your struggle to share openly with your dad onto God. You fear that you will be judged or punished if you share your heart with Him. This is not the case—He knows your heart and loves you unconditionally.

As a daughter, pursuing honesty in communication takes a lot of strength and character. You can only control your actions, so you must choose honesty and hope that your dad receives it well. You can pray to talk openly with your dad, trusting that his love will allow for understanding and listening.

Are there ways a dad and daughter can have more honest communication?

_____
_____
_____
_____
_____
_____
_____
_____
_____
_____
_____
_____
_____
_____
_____
_____
_____
_____
_____
_____
_____
_____
_____
_____

6

Openness

*Pray for us, for we are sure that
we have a clear conscience, desiring to act
honorably in all things.
(Hebrews 13:18 ESV)*

I'm Here for You

I'M GRATEFUL THAT our relationship with God is not always consequential. God is there for us and with us, even when we mess up. He's never absent, despite how we see our situations, despite how we react to our shortcomings, despite how we feel about our struggles. God is always in our midst. In fact, the most common lie that Satan uses to instill fear into us is that God is far away or absent from our presence.

Your daughter also needs your unending presence as a dad. She needs to know that you're there to listen with abandon, not to lend a consequential ear. As a little girl, she may sometimes be afraid of how you might respond to something as simple as spilled milk. But as your daughter grows up, it's important to represent your heavenly Father in your relationship with her. She needs the confidence to know that you are always there for her.

Being there for your daughter will give her the confidence to know her self worth, the strength to chase her dreams, and the ability to nurture her relationship with God. Make sure your daughter knows that you're there for her.

Promise You Won't Get Mad

WHEN I WAS younger, before confessing something I had done wrong, I would plead, "Please, please, please promise me that you won't get mad." I did this as a reflex, knowing that I had messed up but did not want to receive a punishment or consequence for my actions.

I am sure many daughters have made similar pleas with their dads. A confession like this isn't open and honest. If you approach your dad with openness and truth, it will help you to connect through conversation. You won't fear getting in trouble. You will be able to have a better long-term pattern of dialogue.

In your relationship with God, you must also try to be open. Growth can be accomplished only by a willingness to be vulnerable to others. Openness is not simply talking to God or your dad more frequently. It means being more honest when you have dialogue. It means being vulnerable without fearing what the outcome will be. It means having no restraints and the freedom to say what you want or express how you feel. Being open in your conversations is the key to developing a healthy relationship with your dad.

What is holding you back from sharing your heart openly with God?

_____
_____
_____
_____
_____
_____
_____
_____
_____
_____
_____
_____
_____
_____
_____
_____
_____
_____
_____
_____
_____
_____
_____
_____
_____

7

Availability

*Then you will call upon me and come and
pray to me, and I will hear you.
(Jeremiah 29:12 ESV)*

My Door Is Always Open for You

I REMEMBER HEARING little footsteps approaching my office door as I was reading and writing. My little girl just wanted to sit at my feet. She didn't need to talk, and it was a wonderful feeling knowing that just my presence was enough to make her feel loved and important. She remembers those days as well.

As your daughter grows up to become a young woman, the footsteps sometimes become louder and her voice needs to be heard even more. Just because your little girl is becoming a young woman doesn't mean it's time to close the office door. On the contrary, the door needs to be wide open as well as your heart. Your daughter needs to know that whatever happens, in whatever trouble she might be, or how silly the thing she did, your door is always open.

The Bible often uses a door as a metaphor for our relationship with God. He even promises us that if we knock, He will always open it, love on us, and listen. There is no shame, failure, or disappointment that will shut the door with God, or with your daughter. Keep the door open, Dad.

Do You Have Time for Me?

When we talk to God in prayer, He is always there. This availability helps us to know that He loves us and cares for us. I am grateful that my dad modeled availability for me.

Growing up as a Pastor's kid (PK), I knew my dad's schedule was crazy, chaotic, and hectic. My dad gives a lot of time serving our congregation and our family. Even though my dad is very busy, I could always trust that he would make time for me as his daughter. If I needed my dad, he was there. His door was always open for me to talk with him. He is my number one fan, and he showed this by attending my practices, dance recitals, and parent meetings for my activities. The availability of my dad taught me to trust that when I needed him, he would be there for me.

As a daughter, you should go to your dad with your needs. He may be busy, but you need to trust him to make time for you. If he struggles to be available, you can express why his availability matters to you and pray that God will change his heart.

What does being available mean to you?

_____

_____

_____

_____

_____

_____

_____

_____

_____

_____

_____

_____

_____

_____

_____

_____

_____

_____

_____

_____

_____

_____

_____

_____

_____

Section 2

Faith

1

Grace

Let us then with confidence draw near to the throne of grace, that we may receive mercy and find grace to help in time of need.
(Hebrews 4:16 ESV)

Walk with Grace

WHAT IS THE grace of God? Simply put, it is God's favor and kindness toward us. God rains down grace on us all every day. He freely gives us rich blessings, sometimes little things and sometimes big things, all common graces from which we benefit from. But the best grace is that God purchased our freedom and forgave all our sins. This immeasurable gift was given to you when you believed. We didn't work for it, and we didn't even deserve it. What an awesome God!

I try to have a similar attitude of grace toward my daughter. Each morning I have the chance to begin again with God. Likewise, with my daughter, if she makes mistakes, we can always start over with a clean slate. Every new day, hour, and breath is a chance for her to do better and for me to display God's grace for my daughter.

Balancing grace and correction in parenting is something that most of us strive for but feel like we fail at doing. But rather than be anxious about it, look for God's grace. God freely gives us His grace, so we can do the same with our daughter. Pray for God's grace to know when to forgive but still give correction.

Show Me God's Grace

I AM THE oldest child in my family, meaning I was the guinea pig, so all of my dad's parenting efforts toward me were experimental. My parents were making things up as they went along, and the process was not perfect. My dad taught me early on that he was doing his best as a parent, but I would need to extend grace for any parenting mistakes.

Similarly, I needed much grace extended to me. I tend to be naturally clumsy. I would trip and fall down the stairs. I spilled paint all over the whole table. I toppled a flower vase, spilling flowers. I seemed to cause accidents everywhere that I went. My dad recognized that these were unavoidable mistakes and gave me grace.

As a child, you expect your dad to show you forgiveness and grace, but you may sometimes forget to do the same. You need to recognize that your dad is imperfect and tries his best to parent you, but sometimes he gets it wrong. If you are willing to give grace and forgiveness, it will allow you to grow closer to your dad instead of further apart. It also helps you to learn how much grace God gives you, even when you don't deserve it.

*Was there a time you recall when you were
shown undeserved grace?*

_____

_____

_____

_____

_____

_____

_____

_____

_____

_____

_____

_____

_____

_____

_____

_____

_____

_____

_____

_____

_____

_____

_____

2

Covering

*And it is my prayer that your love
may abound more and more, with knowledge and
all discernment, so that you may approve what is
excellent, and so be pure and
blameless for the day of Christ.
(Philippians 1:9–10 ESV)*

I've Got You Covered

WHEN YOUR DAUGHTER is little, one of the most meaningful times of the day is when you tuck her into bed at night. Those are precious memories, and for your daughter, it is reminding her that you have her covered. She can restfully go to sleep knowing that Dad will always be there.

As she grows up, there are so many other ways you can remind her that you've got her covered. Your little girl always needs to know that Dad is covering her in prayer. Praying over your daughter is one of the greatest acts of love you can show her. In this world that is rampant with sin, sickness, and seen and unseen evil, you cannot protect your daughter at every turn, but you can cover her in prayer.

It's not just in prayer that you can cover your daughter. You ought to also cover her in faith and in her walk with God. You're your daughter's greatest spiritual ally, and as she sees you trust God with your life, she too will learn to understand your spiritual covering and gain confidence from it.

Can You Cover Me?

MY DAD WALKS with God in a way that is anointed. He follows the Lord's path, and there's been great protection in that. From a young age, my dad taught me that I have an anointing over my life and that God has a plan for me.

As I have grown older and matured, I have been grateful to realize that my dad's faith has covered me and allowed me to grow in God's promise for my own life. I can see how covered and blessed I am by God, protected from things others have to face without faith.

My dad's faith impacted and covered me through godly guidance and leadership. One day, when I have children, I want to provide them with this same covering—to raise them in faith and teach them God's promises for their lives. I can do this only if I grow in my faith and personal relationship with God. This is your challenge as a daughter: to grasp faith as your own and trust that He has you covered..

*Who are some people that you consistently
cover in prayer together?*

_____
_____
_____
_____
_____
_____
_____
_____
_____
_____
_____
_____
_____
_____
_____
_____
_____
_____
_____
_____
_____
_____
_____
_____
_____

3

Prayer Life

*Now Jesus was praying in a certain place,
and when he finished, one of his disciples
said to him, "Lord, teach us to pray,
as John taught his disciples."
(Luke 11:1 ESV)*

Don't Forget to Pray

IT'S EASY TO remember to pray with your little girl. Prayers with a young child are cute and easy to recite, together. Bedside prayers, dinner prayers, prayers when she is sick—all of these become precious memories. But as your daughter grows into a young woman, sometimes the prayers together don't come as often.

Don't forget to pray. As the life of your growing daughter becomes more complex and challenging, she needs more prayer, not less. Don't let go of prayer and move it to the back burner.

I've always made it a practice to keep praying with and for my daughter. I've made it a discipline to pray unceasingly. Our prayer times together are a rich and important part of our relationship with God and with each other.

As your daughter grows, it's important to pray that she will discover the spiritual gifts and talents that she has been given and use those gifts to bring glory to God. I ask God to use my daughter for His glory. We should pray that God will grant her favor and give her dreams beyond what any of us could even imagine!

What Do I Say?

MY DAD ALWAYS taught me that prayer is crucial to my everyday life. For my family growing up, "The family that prays together stays together" rang true. Prayer was just a regular part of my childhood. I learned to pray before I ate, before I went to sleep, before I participated in activities, and when I had something on my heart.

Prayer is an essential part of my life because it is a central part of my relationship with my dad. He prayed over me constantly. His prayers were a blessing to receive, but it is a much bigger blessing that I have learned to make prayer a part of my daily life. This is a generational legacy that I want to pass on to my own children.

Prayers are not something God hears and then puts into a filing cabinet to lock away forever. Prayer is something that God hears and responds to. Learning how to pray is something that is carried with you always. You can practice this in your own life, whether or not you have a dad that demonstrates prayer in all things. As a daughter, you can set an example, practicing a prayer routine for yourself that will become second nature to you.

Who can you both pray for together?
How can you pray for them?

_____
_____
_____
_____
_____
_____
_____
_____
_____
_____
_____
_____
_____
_____
_____
_____
_____
_____
_____
_____
_____
_____
_____
_____
_____

4

Worship Life

*Let the word of Christ dwell in you richly,
teaching and admonishing one another
in all wisdom, singing psalms and hymns
and spiritual songs, with thankfulness
in your hearts to God.
(Colossians 3:16, ESV)*

Let's Go to Church

"DO I HAVE to go to church, Dad?" Instead of waiting for the question and wrestling with an answer, get ahead of it. Make attending church important with your daughter. Attending church, especially together as a family, is one of the most important things you can do to impact your daughter's life and future.

We were made to worship God. The Bible commands it, and I've seen lives change because of it. All glory and honor rightfully belongs to God. He literally created us so that we would glorify Him. If you don't attend church regularly, you'll fall out of the habit of worshiping God. Suddenly, you'll forget to pray, you'll stop reading your Bible, and church soon becomes no more important than anything else. Don't let your daughter's extracurricular activities become more important than church!

I don't send my wife and children to church; I *bring* them to church. We attend together, worship together, and watch God work inside our family for His glory. It's also a place where we find and bond together with followers of Jesus Christ. Worship is where dads and daughters belong on Sunday morning!

Do I Have To?

A GENERATIONAL LEGACY of church-going is part of my family tradition. I have grown up in church. My parents grew up in church. The parents of my parents grew up in church. As a pastor's daughter, attending church was not a debate for me, yet there were many days when I didn't want to go. Often, I would have preferred to sleep in, take a day off, or hang out with my friends. I think this is a fairly typical teenage response.

Recently I have been thinking about the importance of church for me. As a daughter, seeing my dad's genuine faith and worship has made me want to grow in my own faith. When a dad models faithful worship of God and regular church attendance, it causes a daughter to desire it for herself. It inspires her to embrace the truth of what she sees.

Although your dad's faith can be an excellent example for you, ultimately you must choose if you will follow the path on your own. It is up to you to pursue an individual relationship with Jesus Christ. You need to grow in your faith and worship separately from your dad.

How can a dad and daughter better
prioritize worship in their lives?

_____

_____

_____

_____

_____

_____

_____

_____

_____

_____

_____

_____

_____

_____

_____

_____

_____

_____

_____

_____

_____

_____

_____

5

Vision

*God knows—and he heard things that cannot be
told, which man may not utter.
(2 Corinthians 12:3b–4 ESV)*

Keep Looking

HOW CAN YOU help your daughter become the woman God calls her to be?

I always remind my daughter to stay focused on the horizon, to keep dreaming, and to keep looking. I love her passion, dreams, and her aspirations. But as a young woman, she can become impatient with her dreams, especially when things don't always look the way she wants them to. It's important for her to stay focused on her dream because vision looks beyond the situation.

It's so easy to become discouraged when you're young. The education, the mundane, the routine, the learning, and the financial struggles can be frustrating and even overwhelming. As a dad, you need to remind your daughter that her present circumstances don't determine where she can go; they merely determine where she is now. Remind her of God's bigger picture, the reason why she started, and to maintain discipline and a routine on her way toward her dream.

Pray with her about her dreams. Pray that God will give her a calling greater than she can imagine, greater than even her dad's vision.

Look What I See

THE STOPLIGHT TURNED red, and my dad started speaking. He told me that God had anointed me for great things, that I would be successful, and that God had big plans in store for my life. This didn't just happen once; my dad spoke vision into my life often.

It wasn't just at stoplights that my dad spoke promises over me. We could be at the gas station, a restaurant, on our way to a sporting event, or even gathered around the kitchen table, and my dad would speak life and vision over me. We would joke about the frequency and randomness of these speeches as they could occur anywhere and at any time.

I often brushed off my dad's comments, but eventually, I learned to find the truth they held. My dad had the foresight for my life, which he had gained from years of walking with God. This allowed him to speak a vision over my life. It is my responsibility as a daughter to prayerfully consider these wise lessons and prayerfully apply them to my life.

Your heavenly Father has a vision for your life. Keep looking until you see it.

*Has the Holy Spirit placed a vision
for your lives in your hearts?*

_____

_____

_____

_____

_____

_____

_____

_____

_____

_____

_____

_____

_____

_____

_____

_____

_____

_____

_____

_____

_____

_____

_____

_____

_____

6

Discipleship

*In the same way, let your light shine before others,
so that they may see your good works and give
glory to your Father who is in heaven.
(Matthew 5:16 ESV)*

Walk This Way

WHEN SHE WAS a little girl, Sarah would step into my big shoes, stomp around, and fall down. We'd laugh and she'd try again, and again, and again. Her little feet were swallowed up by my big shoes, but she loved walking in the steps of her dad.

How can you help your daughter walk in your steps later in life? When your little girl turns into a young woman, she still needs her dad's help, to walk in your footsteps while developing her own walk. She may fall and slip along the way of life, just as she did when she was little. But your job as a dad is to be her godly pioneer. Life can be messy sometimes, but it will be less messy if Dad is there to forge a path for her and along with her.

Dad as a discipler means that you "let your light shine" so that others may see God's good work.

It means you both, dad and daughter together, find ways for her light to shine as well. And when you're a dad of honor and integrity, your daughter will walk in the same way.

I Am Following You

MY DAD HAS always set a great example of what a disciple or follower of Christ should look like. He has shown me how to treat others lovingly, how I should walk with Christ, and how I should show God's grace to others.

Although my dad is a pastor, his discipleship to me speaks loudest through his actions. It helps me to understand why I need to draw closer to God as it allows me to see how to better love others. I see him growing in his relationship with Christ, and I learn from that. As he grows closer to God, he can love me more, which grows our relationship as dad and daughter.

Having a dad who disciples you well is a wonderful thing, but there is far greater discipleship when you walk in relationship with your heavenly Father. As a daughter, when you grow in your relationship with God, you can disciple others. Like a dad-daughter relationship, being an example of Christ has to be a team effort in that there is one who leads and one who learns. And many times, as dad and daughter, we learn from one another.

What are some practical ways you can disciple people in your lives?

_____

_____

_____

_____

_____

_____

_____

_____

_____

_____

_____

_____

_____

_____

_____

_____

_____

_____

_____

_____

_____

_____

_____

Section 3

Finances

1

Stewardship

*One who is faithful in a very little is also faithful
in much, and one who is dishonest in
a very little is also dishonest in much.
(Luke 16:10 ESV)*

Secure the Bag

I'VE WATCHED TOO many people waste away their earnings and savings. Those who find a way to make a lot of money quickly are sometimes the worst spenders. I've tried to make it a discipline to show my daughter what it means to "secure the bag."

The Bible instructs us to "save for the future" (Proverbs 21:20) and to "be faithful and wise" (Matthew 24:45) with what God has given us. Stewardship is all about respecting what God has blessed us with. With God's help, I show my daughter with my words and actions how to manage money. I let her see it, plainly and openly.

Generational wealth is something you want to nurture in your family and with your daughter. All too often, girls are sent out into the world with no knowledge of how to steward finances.

Being a good steward is an act of worship and a way for a dad and daughter to grow closer together. As a dad, you can empower your daughter by displaying what it means to be a good steward. Money doesn't bring happiness, and unless she understands money, your daughter can fall into the trap of believing so.

What Do I Do with This?

BEFORE I GOT my first job, I relied on my dad for every penny of spending money. If I needed money, I asked him for it. More often than not, once I received the cash, I blew it immediately. I was not responsible with what I was given, and it would soon be gone—spent on friends, shopping, or food. I didn't know how to handle money with respect.

When I became a lifeguard, I started earning my own money for the first time. This didn't mean I couldn't still splurge occasionally, but it did mean being smarter and not blowing all of my money at once. Before I got my first paycheck, my dad sat me down and spoke with me about the importance of stewardship and handling my money responsibly.

It is crucial that I take care of our money because it is a gift from God, and we should have greater care for what He has entrusted us with. This means being diligent and thoughtful about where we spend our money. It does not matter if you have a lot of money or a little bit; you need to be smart with it. This brings honor to the gift that God has given you.

What is an example of something that you have stewarded well in your life?

_____

_____

_____

_____

_____

_____

_____

_____

_____

_____

_____

_____

_____

_____

_____

_____

_____

_____

_____

_____

_____

_____

_____

2

Money Habits

And if you have not been faithful in that
which is another's, who will give
you that which is your own?
(Luke 16:12 ESV)

Dad

Bring Me Back My Change

WHEN MY DAUGHTER asks me for money
(and as she grows older, this occurs frequently!),
I always ask her to bring me the change back. It's
usually not much, but even if it's a few coins, I
make an effort to get the change back in my
pocket. Why do I insist?

In real life, money does not come easily. You
have to work for it. If your daughter is raised to
believe the earning of money is frivolous and
trouble-free, she'll become a selfish adult who has
learned only to receive. The Bible tells us to "Buy
truth, and do not sell it. Get wisdom and instruction and understanding" (Proverbs 23:23). Your
role as a dad is to display the heavenly Father's
wisdom to your daughter. Your job, even with
money, is to pass on God's desires for how your
daughter ought to manage money throughout
her life.

Your money habits are as important as
worship habits, prayer habits, and faith habits.
Teaching your daughter to value what she
receives from you will open her heart and mind
to how her Father in heaven wants to bless her.

It's My Money

TO HAVE MONEY habits, you have to have money to spend. This means that you have to have an income from somewhere. Whether that money is from the "Bank of Parents" or a job, creating good money habits before you find a source of income is also very necessary. Creating money habits early on makes life so much easier when you have a steady flow of income.

I used to have no clue how to navigate my money, and I would blow it all. I was consistently poor with my money habits until I got a job, and my dad taught me to do be smarter with my spending.

When my dad gave me money without the habits to use it wisely, I wasted it. When my dad taught me how to give part of my paycheck to God, I learned that this act of obedience helped to make the rest of my money habits smarter. I learned how to honor God with my money, treat myself, and save responsibly. I didn't learn these lessons simply by receiving money; I learned them through my dad's teaching.

As a daughter, we often need to seek help in areas of weakness and trust God to help us.

What are some intentional ways that you can glorify God with your finances?

_____

_____

_____

_____

_____

_____

_____

_____

_____

_____

_____

_____

_____

_____

_____

_____

_____

_____

_____

_____

_____

_____

_____

_____

3

Debt

Be not one of those who give pledges,
who put up security for debts.
(Proverbs 22:26 ESV)

Don't Spend It All

THE BIBLE SAYS the borrower is a slave to the lender (Proverb 22:7). Indeed, when debt begins to pile up, it puts the debtor in a terrible position mentally, emotionally, and even spiritually. The stress can be overwhelming. Many of us have made the mistake of taking on too much debt.

Before watching my daughter go into the world, I want her to understand what it means to become a debtor. I don't want her to grow up to pray and beg that God will dig her out or give her an increase over increase. The issue of debt has plagued generations of families, and I'm committed to make sure our family does not become one of them. Our goal is to become free from the bondage of debt, and my calling as a follower of God is to help my daughter stay free!

It's not a sin to borrow, and there are cases when debt is unavoidable, but you want your daughter to understand that it is God's will to avoid the dangers of debt. Managing your money and debt is the key to lifelong financial success. It's not easy, but commit yourself to the journey.

How Much?

I'M JUST A teenager, so thankfully, I don't have too much experience with debt. However, when I got a debit card at the age of thirteen, it seemed as if the gates of heaven opened wide. On one occasion, I used my debit card to buy some last-minute stuff for a dance competition. My card did not decline; however, it showed on my banking app that I had a negative balance in my account. This was such a scary moment for me. It was the first time that I had ever been in debt!

As a teenager, I often think debt is an adult problem that won't come until I'm older. That day, debt slipped up on me so fast that I didn't see it coming. Thankfully, I was able to ask my dad for five dollars. He gave it to me, so I was almost immediately able to get out of debt. But what if that hadn't happened? What if I didn't have a loving resource? I could have easily gotten stuck in a hole I couldn't dig my way out of.

Sin is like that. We owe an unfathomable debt to God that can not be repaid. Thankfully, we have a heavenly Father who paid our debt when He sent Jesus to die in our place. He covered our debt completely.

What are some habits you can develop
to avoid debt?

_____
_____
_____
_____
_____
_____
_____
_____
_____
_____
_____
_____
_____
_____
_____
_____
_____
_____
_____
_____
_____
_____
_____
_____

4

Giving

*Give, and it will be given to you. Good measure,
pressed down, shaken together, running over, will
be put into your lap. For with the measure you use
it will be measured back to you.*
(Luke 6:38 ESV)

Radical Generosity

IF THERE'S ANY single principle the Bible is very clear about, it's "Give and it shall be given to you." Believers and even unbelievers often quote Jesus' words about giving. It reminds me of how my grandmother always told me, "A closed fist never got nothing." She was an example of radical generosity, something I want to pass down to my daughter.

I often share with my daughter how God wants to give us something better, but a part of our faith is making sure that we give back to God. Don't hold onto resources too tightly. Give freely and expect God to bless you. Or stow it all away and watch God's blessings get stowed away.

I pray that God will instill the spirit of generosity in my daughter. I also make it a practice to teach her that when she earns $100, she is actually making $90. As a tither, $90 is kept and $10 is given back to God. Givers become receivers!

It really is true: You can't beat God giving no matter how hard you try.

It's Better to...

I USED TO absolutely hate giving. I saw no point to it. Even though my dad set a great example of giving to his church and others in the community, I saw giving as a way for people to take my money. From my childlike perspective, giving seemed to be a useless activity.

Over my life, I have watched my dad grow and prosper from tithing and giving back to God. This gave me a deeper understanding and value for the true meaning of giving. My dad consistently gives God the first ten percent of all he receives, and God always gives back more.

God grows you through your giving. When you give with a joyful heart, it blesses others, and it blesses you as well; your gift—whether finances, talents, or time—is multiplied when you give. As a daughter, when you seek to give, you will learn the blessings and promises of God's faithfulness.

When you are generous with what you have, God can trust you with more.

Are you a cheerful giver or a reluctant giver?

_____
_____
_____
_____
_____
_____
_____
_____
_____
_____
_____
_____
_____
_____
_____
_____
_____
_____
_____
_____
_____
_____
_____
_____
_____

5

Generational Wealth

And gave their land as a heritage.
For his steadfast love endures forever.
(Psalm 136:21 ESV)

Pass It On

Y O U G I V E Y O U R daughter strength and power with generational wealth. One of your goals as a dad is to instill in her the idea of passing wealth along to future generations. You want your daughter to pass her faith and her wealth along. All too often, the life of a young woman becomes beholden to too much spending, too much debt, and not enough savings. She lives beyond her means.

When your daughter is young, especially when she is a child, she doesn't consider the importance of saving. But it's your job to graduate her from the piggy bank to the real bank, and to instruct her on how to save enough wealth to empower her children and grandchildren. Money ought to be saved and not devoured. If you can instill this in your daughter at a young age, she will remember it throughout the rest of her life.

The Bible talks about the storehouse. God's storehouses are significant because they demonstrate His sovereignty and control over all things. Likewise, you too should build a storehouse and help your daughter to do the same.

I Want It All

MY GRANDMA USED to sit me down and tell me the importance of tithing and saving money so that I will worship God with what I have and create a legacy of wealth for the next generation. I saw my dad also model these principles.

Practically speaking, my dad is building generational wealth to pass on financial blessings to his children. From a spiritual sense, he is establishing something far greater. He has built a legacy of spiritual wealth that will impact our family for generations.

My dad has taught me that whether financial or spiritual, wealth comes from entrusting God with everything. Trusting God should become like a reflex to us—something that we do naturally. This will give us a legacy of wealth to pass on to the next generation.

When we trust God we gain all the Father wants us to have and more.

*What legacy would you like to pass on
to the next generation and why?*

_____

_____

_____

_____

_____

_____

_____

_____

_____

_____

_____

_____

_____

_____

_____

_____

_____

_____

_____

_____

_____

_____

_____

_____

Section 4

Family

1

Love

How precious is your steadfast love, O God!
The children of mankind take refuge in the
shadow of your wings.
(Psalm 36:7 ESV)

Unconditional Love

GOD'S UNCONDITIONAL LOVE does not mean that He loves everything we do, but rather His love is so intense that He loves us even when we fail Him. God's love is very patient and kind, never jealous or envious, never boastful or proud, never haughty or selfish or rude. His love does not demand its own way. It is not irritable or touchy. It does not hold grudges and will hardly even notice when others do it wrong.

Likewise, our love for our daughters should be expressed unconditionally. Our children sometimes fail or disappoint us. Yes, sometimes they are even deceitful as they grow and learn how to live outside of the bubble called "home." But when our little girls grow up, it's important they always feel our unconditional love. There might be times when we're unhappy with their words or actions, and those are the times we need to show them God's unconditional love.

They say a girl's first true love is her dad. Indeed, dads play a big role in their daughters' self-esteem and self-worth, even in their future romantic relationships. So fill your daughter with the same kind of love God gives you, the unconditional kind!

It Never Runs Out

WHEN I WAS a little girl, I couldn't fall asleep without telling my father I loved him. If I didn't say, "I love you," or wish him a good night, I would lie in bed wide-eyed and awake. There was something about sharing love and hearing it reciprocated that brought me peace and rest. To this day, I still tell my dad, "I love you," before I go to sleep and rest reassured when I hear it in return.

Even after a bad day or a fight with my dad, it was essential to exchange "I love you's." My dad taught me that he would always love me, no matter what happened. I knew that I was loved even if I made mistakes, was in a bad mood, or made bad choices. My dad always loves me.

God is love, and His love never runs out. God knows everything about me—the good and the bad—and He still loves me. I am thankful that my dad could model this characteristic of God to me. It taught me that love is not temporary or dependent on anything I can do or earn. It is freely given.

One thing you can be sure of and that is, your heavenly Father will always love you.

How has God displayed His love for you
as a dad and daughter?

_____
_____
_____
_____
_____
_____
_____
_____
_____
_____
_____
_____
_____
_____
_____
_____
_____
_____
_____
_____
_____
_____
_____
_____

2

Gratitude

Give thanks in all circumstances;
for this is the will of God in Christ Jesus for you.
(1 Thessalonians 5:18 ESV)

Say Thank You!

I'M DETERMINED THAT my daughter doesn't grow up and leave our home someday with the spirit of entitlement. We are all sinners, and deserve nothing from God or from the world. The Bible is instructive when Jesus shares that only one healed leper returned to say, "Thank you." Likewise, as a dad and daughter, we are grateful together for everything God does.

How do you express gratitude with your daughter? First, make it a practice to tell her that you are thankful for her. I thank my daughter for who she is, for the gifts and talents God has given to her, and for her faithfulness. I also thank everyone who surrounds my daughter, her friends and family, for how they treat her and respect her. And, I thank God for His favor and continued blessing upon her life.

I challenge you, Dad, to be more thankful with your daughter in actions and words. It's a part of being close with her. It springs from the reality that God does so much for you, and that He is at the center of your relationship.

I Am Grateful!

LIFE IS BUSY. It is easy to take things for granted in the hustle and bustle of our daily lives. We have school, activities, and time with friends, and we often forget to value the people who work hard to keep all of these pieces moving forward.

I sometimes forget to express gratitude to my dad. I assume that he will step in to care for me without recognizing that it takes a lot of effort and sacrifice to be there for me. I expect to have everything I need, yet I often forget to be thankful for what is supplied.

As I matured, I began to recognize how important it is to say, "Thank you." I have learned that it is not enough just to be grateful; I need to express my gratitude.

You need to be thankful for the love of your dad—his time, provision, and care. This thankfulness acknowledges and encourages his efforts. In the same way, God desires your gratitude and praise. He wants you to acknowledge that He provides for your good. He wants you to come to Him with a heart of thanksgiving. This gratefulness will draw you closer to your heavenly Father.

What are three things that you
are grateful for today?

_____

_____

_____

_____

_____

_____

_____

_____

_____

_____

_____

_____

_____

_____

_____

_____

_____

_____

_____

_____

_____

_____

3

Respect

Children, obey your parents in the Lord,
for this is right. "Honor your father and mother"
(this is the first commandment with a promise),
"that it may go well with you and that you may
live long in the land." Fathers, do not provoke
your children to anger, but bring them up in the
discipline and instruction of the Lord.
(Ephesians 6:1–4 ESV)

Honor Your Elders

CHILDREN ARE OFTEN one-sided, even selfish, in their relationships with other people, including with their parents. "What about me?" is something we hear from our children. As my daughter was growing up, however, respect was something that had to be instilled into her. By that I mean respect for me, her mother, and all the other adults in her life.

Respect is a two-way street. I respect my daughter, and I also expect her to respect me, but not out of any sense of ego or self-conceit. Respect is earned by all those who pave the way. We all have pioneers in our lives who sacrificed to make a way. We all have an Abraham or Sarah in our lives, and to forsake them by showing disrespect is both unwise and unbiblical.

Disrespect is the primary root of disobedience. Lying, stealing, vandalism, strife, and disobedience stem from an attitude of disrespect toward someone or something. But when you, as a dad, set a standard of respect in your home, the reward is relationship. Peace reigns and better communication results. We must teach our daughters, honor God and those whom God has placed before you!

It's a Two-Way Street

I WAS ALWAYS taught to respect my elders, teachers, leaders, and especially my parents. My dad showed me how to be respectful to those around me.

My dad also taught me something very wise: that I deserved to be treated with respect. He respected my siblings and me so that when we were put in a situation where we were treated with less than respect, we would be able to communicate that this was unacceptable. We learned loving respect by being treated respectfully.

The fact that my dad showed me respect made me feel loved. It is important that I respect my dad as well to show him love. Through his example, I learned that respecting those around me can demonstrate God's love for them. I want people to see the Lord in me, so I try to practice respect for anyone I interact with.

We should ask ourselves an important question: am I giving the type of respect that I want to receive?

How can a dad and daughter show respectful
behavior toward each other?

_____

_____

_____

_____

_____

_____

_____

_____

_____

_____

_____

_____

_____

_____

_____

_____

_____

_____

_____

_____

_____

_____

_____

_____

4

Togetherness

And above all these put on love, which binds
everything together in perfect harmony.
(Colossians 3:14 ESV)

Let's Stay Together

DON'T LET THE enemy have a more influential voice with your daughter than you do. This is the danger you may face as your daughter begins to grow up. You may sense that your influence is waning, so you will tend to drift away instead of working hard to draw near. Don't give your daughter a reason to say to you, "We're not as close as we used to be."

It's easy to find ways to nurture your dad-daughter relationship when she is a little girl. But it takes purpose and intention as she grows into a young woman. Your calling is to keep the bond close and make a more conscious effort to spend time together, talk, and to pray. Don't wait for the emergencies! With your daughter, treat every single day as an opportunity to draw closer together.

How you spend time with your daughter is a lot like how you spend it with God. It takes effort. If you ignore God, it's hard to be receptive to what He is trying to say to you, right? If you ignore your daughter, the same will hold true. She desires to be close to you, so be a close dad.

I Need You

I FOLLOWED MY dad around like a shadow when I was a little girl. I wanted to be with him and go wherever he went. Most children desire togetherness with their dads. They want to feel connected in a shared sense of belonging.

As you age, you become more independent. This is a good, natural thing. You grow in your identity, which is often very different from that of your dad. Becoming more secure in your independence doesn't mean that there can't be unity in your relationship with your dad. You can grow and mature, focusing on agreement instead of conflict. It is natural for conflicts to arise at this age and stage, but when you spend time together with your dad, he can learn your heart, and you can hear his.

This togetherness creates a unity that allows you the assurance that your dad will be there when you have trials or are facing difficult battles. It helps to deepen your relationship with your dad in the same way that increasing in togetherness with Jesus helps you to know Him better.

Don't be afraid to let your dad hear you say—I need you!

How does unity with God better connect
a dad and daughter?

_____

_____

_____

_____

_____

_____

_____

_____

_____

_____

_____

_____

_____

_____

_____

_____

_____

_____

_____

_____

_____

_____

_____

_____

_____

5

Encouragement

The good person out of the good treasure of his heart produces good, and the evil person out of his evil treasure produces evil, for out of the abundance of the heart his mouth speaks.
(Luke 6:45 ESV)

Speak Life

LIFE AND DEATH are in the power of the tongue. What your tongue produces has eternal implications, for it reveals what is in your heart. Words can build, and they can destroy. Words carry meaning and momentum within yourself and your relationships. Speaking life-giving words can bring love, encouragement, truth, connection, and guidance, and they can even impact your memories.

In the world, your daughter faces words of negativity, hate, prejudice, deceit, and evil. So your job as a dad is to be a constant source of life-giving words to combat the life-killing words she confronts on a daily basis. The Bible says, "For by your words you will be acquitted, and by your words you will be condemned" (Matthew 12:37). Be intentional about when and how you speak life into your daughter.

Being a life-giving dad also means that you have to encourage yourself in the Lord. When I'm feeling down about my own parental decisions or my own personal life, I show my daughter how I encourage myself in the Lord, so that she learns to do the same. Speak life over her and yourself.

Producing Positive Affirmation

WHEN I WAS in eighth grade, my dad drove me to school every day. Each day started with encouragement. He had me repeat affirmations and talk about positives that would happen in my upcoming day. For that short fifteen-minute ride, he helped me to focus on the good things that I was looking forward to and feel encouraged for the week ahead.

As a daughter, you know that your dad's words affect you. You naturally seek positive words from him. This should be a good reminder that you need to go to God's Word for daily encouragement. Imagine how much it would change your daily outlook if you started each day with affirmations from God's Word! You need to spend time in His truth and His promises.

When you spend time in God's Word, it encourages you. This encouragement will allow you to uplift yourself and others. So, I encourage you, to speak life!

How can you intentionally encourage other people, as a dad and daughter?

_____
_____
_____
_____
_____
_____
_____
_____
_____
_____
_____
_____
_____
_____
_____
_____
_____
_____
_____
_____
_____
_____
_____
_____
_____
_____

Section 5

Growing Up

1

Privacy

*But he would withdraw to desolate
places and pray.
(Luke 5:16 ESV)*

I'll Give You Space

GOD DOES NOT intrude on you. He's given you the gift of choice as well as the space and freedom to make your own decisions. He could easily have made you like a robot programmed to do His every bidding, but He didn't, because He made you for the purpose of relationships and love.

Likewise, at times your role as a dad is to give your daughter the space she needs. It's difficult when you watch your daughter become a young woman and the door to your relationship starts to close. You want to barge in! But she's becoming her own person and woman, and you need to learn to be comfortable with the door closing at times. You must learn to knock out of love and respect, just as Jesus knocks on the door of our heart.

If you, as a dad, raise your daughter in the admonishment of the Lord, and if you continue to pray for her, you can better walk the fine line between respect and intrusion. You can trust that your Father in heaven will watch over her and guide her when the door is closed. It's not a separation, and she needs to learn how to use her newfound space responsibly.

Knock Before You Enter

WHEN I WAS little, the door to my room was always open. I would play and sleep with it open. Over time, as I grew older, my door closed more often.

From my dad's perspective, the closed door seemed standoffish. This upset him. He felt that it meant I didn't want to talk or receive anything he was saying. The truth was that I needed some privacy, just like any other teenager. I needed to shut myself in my room and decompress.

I'm sure this aggravated my dad, but it was something that I had learned from him. At the end of the day, whenever he is tired, he goes into his room and closes the door. This is a great mental health habit.

You need time to yourself to recharge and rest. This doesn't mean that you, as a daughter, are closing the door on your childhood. This simply means that you are caring for your needs. Helping your dad see that you need privacy is important. Privacy also allows you to rest and meditate on God's Word. In the Bible, Jesus set an excellent example for this when He would withdraw from crowds to pray and recharge.

*How can we be more intentional about spending
private time alone with God?*

_____

_____

_____

_____

_____

_____

_____

_____

_____

_____

_____

_____

_____

_____

_____

_____

_____

_____

_____

_____

_____

_____

2

Dating

*The beginning of wisdom is this: Get wisdom,
and whatever you get, get insight.
(Proverbs 4:7 ESV)*

I Want the Best for You

YOUR ROLE IN interacting with your daughter provides the closest, real-life human example of how she interacts with God. You can be the best example of how God is strong and protective, loving and gentle, knowledgeable and trustworthy. When your daughter begins to mature and develop her own dating relationships, it's even more important that you continue to mirror God in your relationship with her.

It's a complicated and scary task, and it needs to be steeped in prayer. Your best efforts will be incomplete and imperfect, but that's to be expected. You might sometimes be at odds with your daughter and contend with her relationship choices. But you must not give up on your responsibility to guide her into healthy and godly relationships, and you must also be willing to give her the space she needs to learn.

You need to value your daughter's femaleness, her own perspectives, her emotions, and her strong-spirited will. You know that your daughter can be tough as nails one minute and soft as a pillow or cute as a button the next. You want the best for your daughter, and in your prayers and actions, you offer both respect and guidance.

Who Am I Looking For?

AS CRAZY AS it sounds, I think that my dad gives the best relationship advice in the entire world. Once I discovered dating, I realized I had no clue what I was looking for or how to navigate this alone.

When I had dating questions, I often asked my friends or sister for advice, and they gave opinions, but it wasn't backed by wise life experience. When I went to my dad for advice, he always had a great perspective. This taught me that before I ask for advice, I had to make sure that the people I'm asking have a relationship with God and my best interests at heart.

I am thankful that God speaks to me through my dad. He has had valuable experience backed with biblical truth. This has strengthened my walk with God regarding relationships because I learned what the Bible says. It also allows me to ask questions and learn what the Bible says about my circumstance: *What does God's Word say about seasons of waiting? What does God say about marriage?* My dad's advice has always pointed back to the Word, which is precisely what I need. As we put our relationship with God first, it allows us to pursue healthy relationships with others.

What is God's Word teaching you
about dating?

_____

_____
_____
_____
_____
_____
_____
_____
_____
_____
_____
_____
_____
_____
_____
_____
_____
_____
_____
_____
_____
_____
_____
_____
_____

3

Future

Fathers, do not provoke your children,
lest they become discouraged.
(Colossians 3:21 ESV)

You Can Do Anything!

I LOVE REMINDING my daughter how the Bible says, "Now to him who is able to do immeasurably more than all we ask or imagine, according to his power that is at work within us" (Ephesians 3:20). This is a constant reminder to her that she can dream big and do anything her heart desires!

God's purposes are greater than ours. His ways are not our ways, and His thoughts are not our thoughts. He is God; we are not. He does things in infinite ways that we don't know to even ask for. He knows us better than we know ourselves. So I try not to limit my daughter's expectations for how God will use her. I pray that she will surpass me in everything she does.

When I held my daughter for the first time, I could not believe God would bless me in such a way. So, I decided I would become my daughter's biggest cheerleader. I would insist that she love and believe in herself, and I would expose her to things and people who would help make her dreams possible. Dad, pray big prayers to God. He can do anything!

It's My Life

MY DAD LOVES his college. He used to take our family on tours there. The closer I got to college age, my dad became more annoyingly persistent in his efforts to convince me to attend the sister school of his alma mater. He would flood me with merchandise or memorabilia that I refused to wear.

I rebelled against all of this. My dad's intentions for me were good—he wanted me to experience what he loved, but he went about it the wrong way. It felt as if he wanted to live vicariously through me, and I finally had to tell him, "Let me live my own life!"

Gratefully, my dad listened to my perspective and backed off. He felt that his college choice for me was where God would lead me, but he realized that it wasn't his job to convince me. Setting boundaries with my dad was an important step for me. It also gave me the space to prayerfully consider my options and opinions. My dad respecting that boundary was crucial in allowing me to seek what God had for me. In the end, I chose the sister school to my dad's alma mater, but now I know that is where God is leading me instead of feeling pressured by my dad.

Do you trust God with His plans
for your future?

_____

_____

_____

_____

_____

_____

_____

_____

_____

_____

_____

_____

_____

_____

_____

_____

_____

_____

_____

_____

_____

_____

_____

4

Guidance

Whoever walks with the wise becomes wise,
but the companions of fools will suffer harm.
(Proverbs 13:20 ESV)

Read the Signs

I OFTEN TELL my daughter she can go anywhere in the world if she just reads the signs. My job as her dad is to help her look for and understand the signs. God gives us direction according to His Word and through prayer. This is how He gives us signs and a beautiful roadmap. He will point my daughter in the right direction if she just learns to read the signs.

What happens when we misread the signs, or if we forget about God and try to live life by our own signs?

I often use a navigation app when I'm driving with my daughter. Sometimes I forget to listen to it, or sometimes I might get a little off track. When I do, it tells me to make a U-turn. Then when we turn the car back around, we're fast on our way to our destination. No harm has been done, and we've wasted only a little time.

This reminds me of how we sometimes get off track with God. We take matters into our own hands and end up getting lost. Part of your role as a dad is to help your daughter understand that it's OK to take a U-turn. It's a part of life. And when she does, God will give her direction, and redirection, according to His will for her.

Point Me in the Right Direction

LIKE MANY TEENAGERS, I've gone through plenty of different personality phases. Ultimately, these phases have been directly related to who I am hanging out with. Sometimes those friends were not the best reflection of what my life was destined for. Without even realizing it, the wrong friends can begin to change you negatively. It isn't a flip of the switch; it is a slow process of change.

One day, my dad sat me down and told me he was concerned about me. I had been hanging around with the wrong people, which changed me. I was doing things out of character, and bad choices filled my actions and behavior. Truthfully, I had dissociated with who God called me to be. I didn't listen to a single word that my dad said. I took his guidance and threw it in the trash.

I didn't want to hear what my dad had to say, but I definitely needed to hear it. Looking back, I realize that he was so right. In the same way, God speaks to us in His Word or through other people to call us back when we have stepped away from Him. It may not be what we want to hear, but following the Lord's guidance brings us to a place of peace and protection in the same way.

What is something in your life that you are
seeking guidance for?

_____

_____

_____

_____

_____

_____

_____

_____

_____

_____

_____

_____

_____

_____

_____

_____

_____

_____

_____

_____

_____

_____

_____

_____

5

Support

When I thought, "My foot slips,"
your steadfast love, O Lord, held me up.
(Psalm 94:18 ESV)

I've Got Your Back

WHEN MY DAUGHTER was in kindergarten and I dropped her off at school, she would always look back to see if I was still there. I was her rock, her confidence, and the person she looked to for security and support. It was precious, and I still treasure that memory. She does as well.

As your daughter grows up, she still has to know that you support her at all times. It doesn't matter if she's five or fifteen years old, she needs to know you're there for her. As she grows up, she needs and demands her independence. But that doesn't mean she won't continue to need your support. In the same way, God gives you your own free will and independence, but He never forsakes you. He's always there when you need Him.

Your daughter will develop a strong sense of empowerment if she has the fullest of confidence that her dad loves and cares for her. It's no different from how you develop confidence as a result of God's unending and merciful love for you. That's what keeps you going in tough times. God has your back, and you have your daughter's back.

Just Support Me, Please

WHAT IS MY purpose? What am I put on this planet for? Who am I? What are my gifts? I would often wonder what the answers were to these questions. I did my best to find out by signing up to try various activities. I started with baseball, switched to basketball, then tried soccer, dance, gymnastics, tennis, cello, broadcasting, cheerleading, computer programming, and various other interests.

Most of these activities didn't stick, but as I tried one thing after another, my dad always supported me. Whenever I asked to try another activity, he would say, "Yes." My dad loved me enough to support me as I tried to figure out what fit me best. He also allowed me to be honest and express that I was still trying to figure things out.

The fact that my dad supported me in whatever I tried gave me the confidence to begin to learn who God made me to be. It also helped my dad to see what areas I was gifted in or found joy in pursuing. It helped us both figure out the direction in which God was leading me. This support was critical to learning my identity in Christ.

What is an area in your life that you wish that
you had more support in?

_____

_____

_____

_____

_____

_____

_____

_____

_____

_____

_____

_____

_____

_____

_____

_____

_____

_____

_____

_____

_____

_____

_____

_____

_____

6

Dream Big!

For I know the plans I have for you,
declares the Lord, plans for welfare and not for
evil, to give you a future and a hope.
(Jeremiah 29:11 ESV)

Dream Big, Daughter!

GOD DOESN'T EVER want us to dream small. And he especially wants us, as dads, to teach our daughters how to dream big! Whatever our daughters dreams are, God wants them to pursue their dreams with great faith and trust. God also wants us to pray for His will and His plans for their lives to be pursued.

What do we tell our daughters about their dreams? The big dreams God wants for us will demand everything from them. They will require boldness and immense faith because at times, their dreams might seem impossible. They will require that she grow in faith, hope, and love. Also, they can have confidence that God is rooting for them and helping—no matter the challenges. Pursuing her big dreams may be hard at times, and there is no guarantee that she will fulfill them. But if she stays close to Christ and keeps dreaming, we can have the fullest of hope that God will be with her and help her to pursue a life of adventure and meaning.

Take heart, encourage your daughter to offer her big dreams to the Lord, and remember that all things are possible with God who loves us!

No Limits

MY DAD OFTEN emphasized two guidelines when I was growing up. The first one was "Never give up," and the second was "Always chase my dreams." I will carry these with me for the rest of my life and pass them down to my children. I truly think that these are principles that have made me who I am today.

I would often feel discouraged, as if my dreams were out of reach. My dad would offer subtle encouragement and motivation to chase what I wanted. He always knew what to say to keep me going.

My dad taught me that God's vision for my life is greater than anything I can understand. This taught me that God's plan is so much larger than anything that I can imagine for myself. If my dad, who loves me, can see a much bigger future for my life, then imagine how much bigger God's plan is for me.

God is also writing a story for you that is filled with purpose. God loves you, His daughter, and His desires are for your good.

*Has God placed a big dream or vision
in your heart?*

_____
_____
_____
_____
_____
_____
_____
_____
_____
_____
_____
_____
_____
_____
_____
_____
_____
_____
_____
_____
_____
_____
_____
_____

7

Closer to Him

He who dwells in the shelter of the Most High will
abide in the shadow of the Almighty.
(Psalm 91:1 ESV)

The Perfect Father

I TRY HARD to be the perfect dad. I pour myself into my little girl, and as she grows into a young woman, I sometimes look back and wonder if I've made the right decisions. Did I say the right things? Did I do the right things? Self-doubt creeps in, and I pray for God to help me be a better dad.

But when I do pray, God reminds me that there is only one Perfect Father. Our Heavenly Father is all-knowing, has all power, and is a God of perfect mercy, kindness, and love. Even though we "do not know the meaning of all things," we can find peace in the sure knowledge that He loves my daughter and me. I might make a mistake, but my daughter is in the hands of the Perfect Father.

Rest in the peace and security that whatever mistakes we make as dads, our daughters belong to the Most High God. He alone carries the burden, and He will guide our daughters according to His perfect will.

A Chosen Daughter

MY DAD AND I have a close relationship because we work on it. We spend time doing things together, which draws us closer. We have a friendship because we pour in time to what we value. We value our relationship, and as a result, it grows.

I recognize that this is unique and that you may not have a close relationship with your dad, which can be a point of great pain and tenderness. You may have done everything you can to achieve your dad's affection, but he fails to provide it. This is not your fault and is not a burden that God wants you to bear.

I hope you and your dad will grow closer through daily devotionals and God's Word, but if that is not the case, you are not without a Father.

God is the perfect Father. Where others fail, He is sovereign. He is with you when you feel abandoned and when your heart seems broken. He is a healer in a time of hurt. He is calling you. God has chosen you as His daughter and will cherish you in beautiful comfort. Draw closer to Him. He is waiting.

What is a practical way that you can work to
intentionally grow closer to God?

_____

_____

_____

_____

_____

_____

_____

_____

_____

_____

_____

_____

_____

_____

_____

_____

_____

_____

_____

_____

_____

_____

_____

_____

_____

To contact the authors or for more information,
visit www.timothywsloan.com.

Social Media for Timothy W. Sloan:

Instagram: @timothysloan
Facebook: @timothywsloan
Twitter: @timothysloan

Social Media for Sarah Sloan:

Instagram: @sarahsloaan

9 781956 267952